HAL·LEONARD

JAZZ PLAY ALONG®

Book and CD for Bb, Eb and C Instruments

Arranged and Produced
by Mark Taylor & Jim Roberts

volume 53

RHYTHM Changes

10 Classic Tunes

ISBN 0-634-09082-8

HAL·LEONARD® CORPORATION

7777 W. BLUEMOUND RD. P.O. BOX 13819 MILWAUKEE, WI 53213

Visit Hal Leonard Online at
www.halleonard.com

Rhythm Changes

Volume 53

Arranged and Produced by
Mark Taylor & Jim Roberts

Featured Players:

Graham Breedlove–Trumpet
John Desalme–Saxophones
Tony Nalker–Piano
Jim Roberts–Bass
Steve Fidyk–Drums

Recorded at Bias Studios, Springfield, Virginia
Bob Dawson, Engineer

HOW TO USE THE CD:

Each song has <u>two</u> tracks:

1) Split Track/Melody

Woodwind, Brass, Keyboard, and **Mallet Players** can use this track as a learning tool for melody style and inflection.

Bass Players can learn and perform with this track – remove the recorded bass track by turning down the volume on the LEFT channel.

Keyboard and **Guitar Players** can learn and perform with this track – remove the recorded piano part by turning down the volume on the RIGHT channel.

2) Full Stereo Track

Soloists or **Groups** can learn and perform with this accompaniment track with the RHYTHM SECTION only.

CELIA

BY EARL "BUD" POWELL

CD
- ◆1 : SPLIT TRACK/MELODY
- ◆2 : FULL STEREO TRACK

C VERSION

CHASING THE BIRD

CD

3 : SPLIT TRACK/MELODY
4 : FULL STEREO TRACK

C VERSION

BY CHARLIE PARKER

COTTON TAIL

BY Duke Ellington

C VERSION

D.C. AL FINE
LAST TIME – WITH REPEAT

(BACK TO ✱ 2 MORE TIMES FOR SOLOS)

CRAZEOLOGY

BY BENNIE HARRIS

C VERSION

FOX HUNT

BY J.J. JOHNSON

I GOT RHYTHM

MUSIC AND LYRICS BY GEORGE GERSHWIN
AND IRA GERSHWIN

NO MOE

CD

13: SPLIT TRACK/MELODY

14: FULL STEREO TRACK

BY SONNY ROLLINS

C VERSION   MEDIUM

OLEO

CD
15: SPLIT TRACK/MELODY
16: FULL STEREO TRACK

C VERSION

BY SONNY ROLLINS

RED CROSS

CD
17 : SPLIT TRACK/MELODY
18 : FULL STEREO TRACK

BY CHARLIE PARKER

C VERSION

STEEPLECHASE

CELIA

❶ : SPLIT TRACK/MELODY
❷ : FULL STEREO TRACK

BY EARL "BUD" POWELL

Bb VERSION   MED. SWING

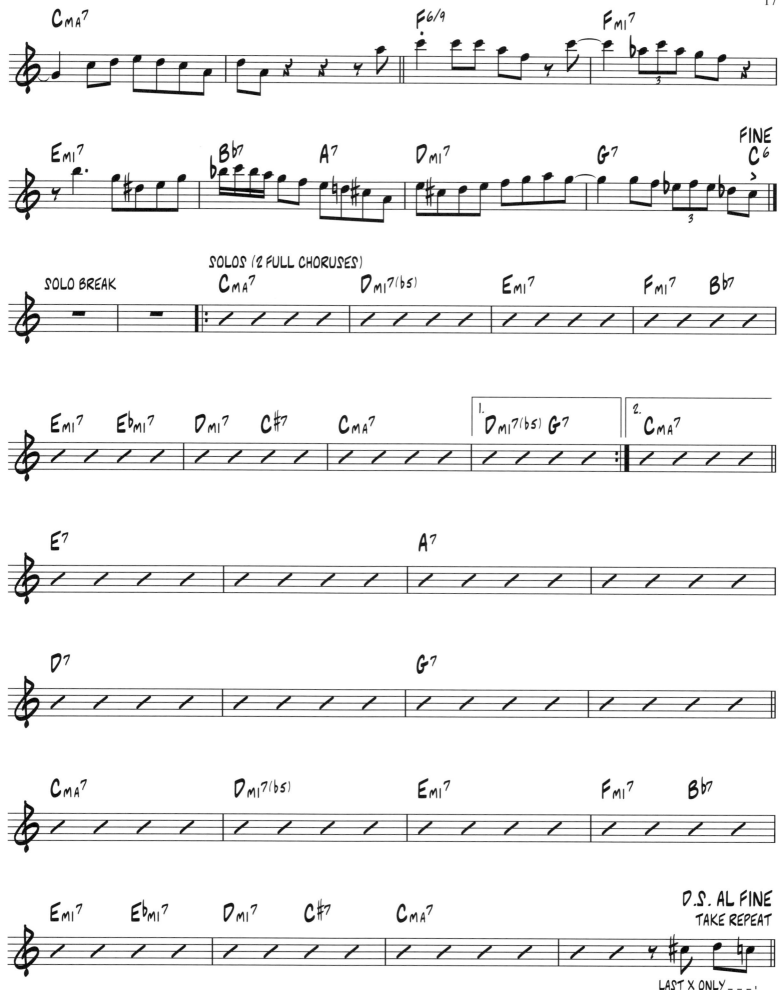

CHASING THE BIRD

BY CHARLIE PARKER

CD
3: SPLIT TRACK/MELODY
4: FULL STEREO TRACK

Bb VERSION   MEDIUM

FINE

SOLO BREAK

SOLOS (3 FULL CHORUSES)

D.C. AL FINE
TAKE REPEAT

COTTON TAIL

BY DUKE ELLINGTON

Bb VERSION

SWING

SOLOS

D.C. AL FINE
LAST TIME – WITH REPEAT

(BACK TO ✳ 2 MORE TIMES FOR SOLOS)

CRAZEOLOGY

BY BENNIE HARRIS

FOX HUNT

Bb VERSION   FAST

BY J.J. JOHNSON

CD

🔟 : SPLIT TRACK/MELODY
🔢 : FULL STEREO TRACK

I GOT RHYTHM

MUSIC AND LYRICS BY GEORGE GERSHWIN
AND IRA GERSHWIN

Bb VERSION

NO MOE

CD
13 : SPLIT TRACK/MELODY
14 : FULL STEREO TRACK

BY SONNY ROLLINS

OLEO

B♭ VERSION

BY SONNY ROLLINS

SOLOS (4 CHORUSES)

FINE

D.C. AL FINE
TAKE REPEAT

Red Cross

BY CHARLIE PARKER

SOLOS (4 FULL CHORUSES)

Steeplechase

BY CHARLIE PARKER

CELIA

BY EARL "BUD" POWELL

CHASING THE BIRD

BY CHARLIE PARKER

COTTON TAIL

BY DUKE ELLINGTON

Eb VERSION

CRAZEOLOGY

BY BENNIE HARRIS

Eb VERSION

FOX HUNT

I GOT RHYTHM

MUSIC AND LYRICS BY GEORGE GERSHWIN
AND IRA GERSHWIN

NO MOE

BY SONNY ROLLINS

E♭ VERSION

OLEO

BY SONNY ROLLINS

Red Cross

BY CHARLIE PARKER

Steeplechase

CELIA

BY EARL "BUD" POWELL

CD
 : SPLIT TRACK/MELODY
2 : FULL STEREO TRACK

𝄢 C VERSION

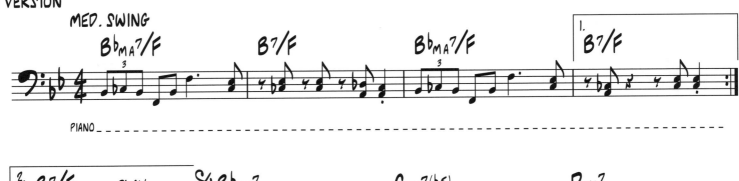

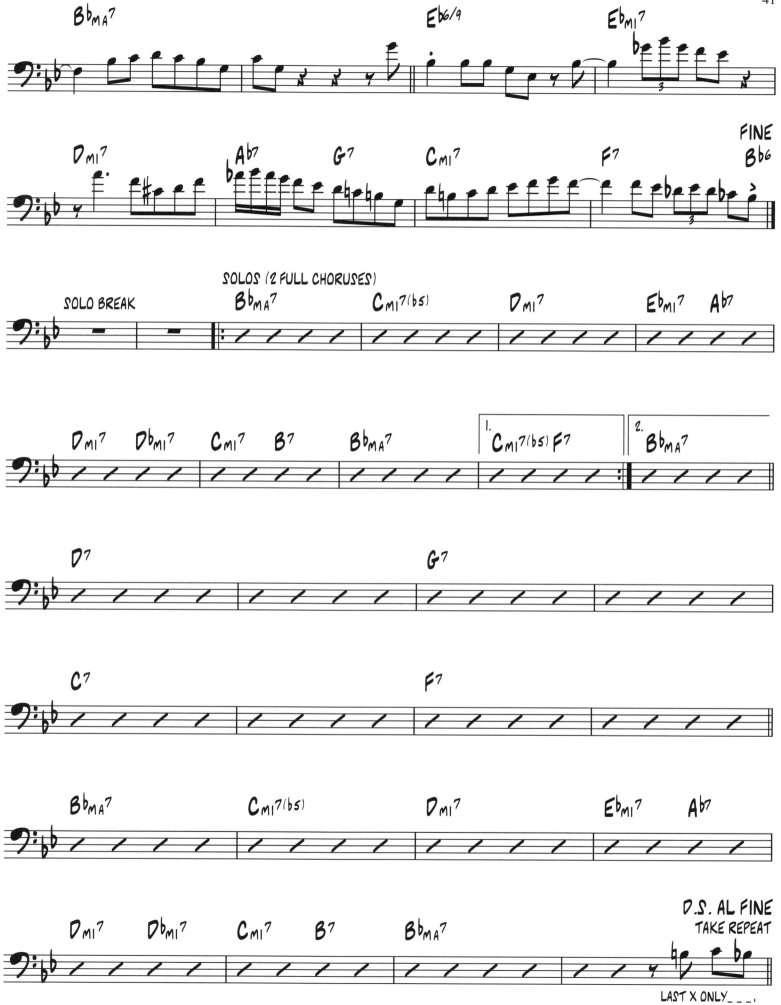

CHASING THE BIRD

BY CHARLIE PARKER

COTTON TAIL

BY DUKE ELLINGTON

CRAZEOLOGY

BY BENNIE HARRIS

FOX HUNT

𝄢 C VERSION   FAST

BY J.J. JOHNSON

I GOT RHYTHM

MUSIC AND LYRICS BY GEORGE GERSHWIN
AND IRA GERSHWIN

C VERSION

NO MOE

BY SONNY ROLLINS

CD
- **13**: SPLIT TRACK/MELODY
- **14**: FULL STEREO TRACK

♪: C VERSION

OLEO

BY SONNY ROLLINS

RED CROSS

BY CHARLIE PARKER

STEEPLECHASE

BY CHARLIE PARKER

ARTIST TRANSCRIPTIONS

Artist Transcriptions are authentic, note-for-note transcriptions of the hottest artists in jazz, pop, and rock today. These outstanding, accurate arrangements are in an easy-to-read format which includes all essential lines. Artist Transcriptions can be used to perform, sequence or reference.

GUITAR & BASS

George Benson
00660113 Guitar Style of $14.95

Pierre Bensusan
00699072 Guitar Book of.................$19.95

Ron Carter
00672331 Acoustic Bass.................$16.95

Stanley Clarke
00672307 The Collection.................$19.95

Al Di Meola
00604041 Cielo E Terra $14.95
00660115 Friday Night in
        San Francisco...............$14.95
00604043 Music, Words, Pictures....$14.95

Tal Farlow
00673245 Jazz Style of $19.95

Bela Fleck and the Flecktones
00672359 Melody/Lyrics/Chords......$18.95

Frank Gambale
00672336 Best of $22.95

Jim Hall
00699389 Jazz Guitar Environments ..$19.95
00699306 Exploring Jazz Guitar $17.95

Allan Holdsworth
00604049 Reaching for the
        Uncommon Chord $14.95

Leo Kottke
00699215 Eight Songs $14.95

Wes Montgomery
00675536 Guitar Transcriptions $17.95

Joe Pass
00672353 The Collection.................$18.95

John Patitucci
00673216 ....$14.95

Django Reinhardt
00027083 Anthology $14.95
00026711 The Genius of $10.95
00026715 A Treasury of Songs $12.95

Johnny Smith
00672374 Guitar Solos $16.95

Mike Stern
00673224 Guitar Book......................$16.95

Mark Whitfield
00672320 Guitar Collection..............$19.95

Gary Willis
00672337 The Collection.................$19.95

SAXOPHONE

Julian "Cannonball" Adderley
00673244 The Collection.................$19.95

Michael Brecker
00673237 ....$19.95
00672429 The Collection.................$19.95

The Brecker Brothers
00672351 And All Their Jazz...........$19.95
00672447 Best of $19.95

Benny Carter
00672314 The Collection.................$22.95
00672315 Plays Standards $22.95

James Carter
00672394 The Collection.................$19.95

John Coltrane
00672494 A Love Supreme..............$12.95
00672529 Giant Steps.....................$14.95
00672493 Plays Coltrane Changes..$19.95
00672349 Plays Giant Steps $19.95
00672453 Plays Standards $19.95
00673233 Solos...............................$22.95

Paul Desmond
00672328 The Collection.................$19.95
00672454 Standard Time $19.95

Kenny Garrett
00672530 The Collection.................$19.95

Stan Getz
00699375 ....$18.95
00672377 Bossa Novas $19.95
00672375 Standards........................$17.95

Coleman Hawkins
00672523 The Collection.................$19.95

Joe Henderson
00672330 Best of $22.95
00673252 Selections from Lush Life
        & So Near So Far $19.95

Kenny G
00673239 Best of $19.95
00673229 Breathless.......................$19.95
00672462 Classics in the Key of G ..$19.95
00672485 Faith: A Holiday Album....$14.95
00672373 The Moment $19.95
00672516 Paradise $14.95

Joe Lovano
00672326 The Collection.................$19.95

Jackie McLean
00672498 The Collection.................$19.95

James Moody
00672372 The Collection $19.95

Frank Morgan
00672416 The Collection.................$19.95

Sonny Rollins
00672444 The Collection.................$19.95

David Sanborn
00675000 The Collection.................$16.95

Bud Shank
00672528 The Collection.................$19.95

Wayne Shorter
00672498 New Best of $19.95

Lew Tabackin
00672455 The Collection.................$19.95

Stanley Turrentine
00672334 The Collection.................$19.95

Lester Young
00672524 The Collection.................$19.95

PIANO & KEYBOARD

Monty Alexander
00672338 The Collection.................$19.95
00672487 Plays Standards $19.95

Kenny Barron
00672318 The Collection.................$22.95

Count Basie
00672520 The Collection.................$19.95

Warren Bernhardt
00672364 The Collection.................$19.95

Cyrus Chesnut
00672439 The Collection.................$19.95

Billy Childs
00673242 The Collection.................$19.95

Chick Corea
00672300 Paint the World $12.95

Bill Evans
00672537 At Town Hall $16.95
00672365 The Collection.................$19.95
00672425 Piano Interpretations........$19.95
00672510 Trio, Vol. 1: 1959-1961 ....$24.95
00672511 Trio, Vol. 2: 1962-1965 ....$24.95
00672512 Trio, Vol. 3: 1968-1974 ....$24.95
00672513 Trio, Vol. 4: 1979-1980 ....$24.95

Benny Goodman
00672492 The Collection.................$16.95

Benny Green
00672329 The Collection.................$19.95

Vince Guaraldi
00672486 The Collection.................$19.95

Herbie Hancock
00672419 The Collection.................$19.95

Gene Harris
00672446 The Collection.................$19.95

Hampton Hawes
00672438 The Collection.................$19.95

Ahmad Jamal
00672322 The Collection.................$22.95

CLARINET

Buddy De Franco
00672423 The Collection.................$19.95

FLUTE

Eric Dolphy
00672379 The Collection.................$19.95

James Moody
00672372 The Collection $19.95

James Newton
00660108 Improvising Flute $14.95

Lew Tabackin
00672455 The Collection.................$19.95

TROMBONE

J.J. Johnson
00672332 The Collection.................$19.95

Brad Mehldau
00672476 The Collection.................$19.95

Thelonious Monk
00672388 Best of $19.95
00672389 The Collection.................$19.95
00672390 Jazz Standards, Vol. 1 ....$19.95
00672391 Jazz Standards, Vol. 2 ....$19.95
00672392 Intermediate Piano Solos..$14.95

Jelly Roll Morton
00672433 The Piano Rolls.............$12.95

Oscar Peterson
00672531 Plays Duke Ellington........$19.95
00672534 Very Best of $19.95

Michael Petrucciani
00673226 ....$17.95

Bud Powell
00672371 Classics $19.95
00672376 The Collection.................$19.95

André Previn
00672437 The Collection.................$19.95

Gonzalo Rubalcaba
00672507 The Collection.................$19.95

Horace Silver
00672303 The Collection.................$19.95

Art Tatum
00672316 The Collection.................$22.95
00672355 Solo Book $19.95

Billy Taylor
00672357 The Collection.................$24.95

McCoy Tyner
00673215 ....$16.95

Cedar Walton
00672321 The Collection.................$19.95

Kenny Werner
00672519 The Collection.................$19.95

Teddy Wilson
00672434 The Collection.................$19.95

TRUMPET

Louis Armstrong
00672480 The Collection.................$14.95
00672481 Plays Standards $14.95

Chet Baker
00672435 The Collection.................$19.95

Randy Brecker
00673234 ....$17.95

The Brecker Brothers
00672351 And All Their Jazz...........$19.95
00672447 Best of $19.95

Miles Davis
00672448 Originals, Vol. 1 ....$19.95
00672451 Originals, Vol. 2 ....$19.95
00672450 Standards, Vol. 1 ....$19.95
00672449 Standards, Vol. 2 ....$19.95

Dizzy Gillespie
00672479 The Collection.................$19.95

Freddie Hubbard
00673214 ....$14.95

Tom Harrell
00672382 Jazz Trumpet Solos $19.95

Chuck Mangione
00672506 The Collection.................$19.95

The Best Selling Jazz Book of All Time Is Now Legal!

The Real Books are the most popular jazz books of all time. Since the 1970s, musicians have trusted these volumes to get them through every gig, night after night. The problem is that the books were illegally produced and distributed, without any regard to copyright law, or royalties paid to the composers who created these musical masterpieces.

Hal Leonard is very proud to present the first legitimate and legal editions of these books ever produced. You won't even notice the difference, other than all the notorious errors being fixed: the covers and typeface look the same, the song lists are nearly identical, and the price for our edition is even cheaper than the originals!

Every conscientious musician will appreciate that these books are now produced accurately and ethically, benefitting the songwriters that we owe for some of the greatest tunes of all time!

VOLUME 1

Includes: Autumn Leaves • Black Orpheus • Bluesette • Body and Soul • Don't Get Around Much Anymore • Falling in Love with Love • Footprints • Giant Steps • Have You Met Miss Jones? • Lullaby of Birdland • Misty • Satin Doll • Stella by Starlight • and hundreds more!

00240221	C Edition	$25.00
00240224	B♭ Edition	$25.00
00240225	E♭ Edition	$25.00
00240226	Bass Clef Edition	$25.00

VOLUME 2

Includes: Avalon • Birdland • Come Rain or Come Shine • Fever • Georgia on My Mind • It Might as Well Be Spring • Moonglow • The Nearness of You • On the Sunny Side of the Street • Route 66 • Sentimental Journey • Smoke Gets in Your Eyes • Tangerine • Yardbird Suite • and more!

00240222	C Edition	$25.00

Coming soon:

00240227	B♭ Edition	$29.95
00240228	E♭ Edition	$29.95
00240229	Bass Clef Edition	$29.95

FOR MORE INFORMATION, SEE YOUR LOCAL MUSIC DEALER, OR WRITE TO:

HAL•LEONARD®
CORPORATION
7777 W. BLUEMOUND RD. P.O. BOX 13819 MILWAUKEE, WI 53213

Complete song lists online at www.halleonard.com

Prices and availability subject to change without notice.

Jazz Instruction & Improvisation

Books for All Instruments from Hal Leonard

AN APPROACH TO JAZZ IMPROVISATION
by Dave Pozzi
Musicians Institute Press
Explore the styles of Charlie Parker, Sonny Rollins, Bud Powell and others with this comprehensive guide to jazz improvisation. Covers: scale choices • chord analysis • phrasing • melodies • harmonic progressions • more.
00695135 Book/CD Pack $17.95

BUILDING A JAZZ VOCABULARY
By Mike Steinel
A valuable resource for learning the basics of jazz from Mike Steinel of the University of North Texas. It covers: the basics of jazz • how to build effective solos • a comprehensive practice routine • and a jazz vocabulary of the masters.
00849911 ....$19.95

THE CYCLE OF FIFTHS
by Emile and Laura De Cosmo
This essential instruction book provides more than 450 exercises, including hundreds of melodic and rhythmic ideas. The book is designed to help improvisors master the cycle of fifths, one of the primary progressions in music. Guaranteed to refine technique, enhance improvisational fluency, and improve sight-reading!
00311114 ....$14.95

THE DIATONIC CYCLE
by Emile and Laura De Cosmo
Renowned jazz educators Emile and Laura De Cosmo provide more than 300 exercises to help improvisors tackle one of music's most common progressions: the diatonic cycle. This book is guaranteed to refine technique, enhance improvisational fluency, and improve sight-reading!
00311115 ....$16.95

EAR TRAINING
by Keith Wyatt, Carl Schroeder and Joe Elliott
Musicians Institute Press
Covers: basic pitch matching • singing major and minor scales • identifying intervals • transcribing melodies and rhythm • identifying chords and progressions • seventh chords and the blues • modal interchange, chromaticism, modulation • and more.
00695198 Book/2-CD Pack....................$19.95

EXERCISES AND ETUDES FOR THE JAZZ INSTRUMENTALIST
by J.J. Johnson
Designed as study material and playable by any instrument, these pieces run the gamut of the jazz experience, featuring common and uncommon time signatures and keys, and styles from ballads to funk. They are progressively graded so that both beginners and professionals will be challenged by the demands of this wonderful music.
00842018 Bass Clef Edition.................$16.95
00842042 Treble Clef Edition $16.95

JAZZOLOGY
THE ENCYCLOPEDIA OF JAZZ THEORY FOR ALL MUSICIANS
by Robert Rawlins and Nor Eddine Bahha
This comprehensive resource covers a variety of jazz topics, for beginners and pros of any instrument. The book serves as an encyclopedia for reference, a thorough methodology for the student, and a workbook for the classroom.
00311167 ....$17.95

JAZZ THEORY RESOURCES
by Bert Ligon
Houston Publishing, Inc.
This is a jazz theory text in two volumes. **Volume 1 includes:** review of basic theory • rhythm in jazz performance • triadic generalization • diatonic harmonic progressions and analysis • substitutions and turnarounds • and more. **Volume 2 includes:** modes and modal frameworks • quartal harmony • extended tertian structures and triadic superimposition • pentatonic applications • coloring "outside" the lines and beyond • and more.
00030458 Volume 1 ....$39.95
00030459 Volume 2 ....$29.95

JOY OF IMPROV
by Dave Frank and John Amaral
This book/CD course on improvisation for all instruments and all styles will help players develop monster musical skills! **Book One** imparts a solid basis in technique, rhythm, chord theory, ear training and improv concepts. **Book Two** explores more advanced chord voicings, chord arranging techniques and more challenging blues and melodic lines. The CD can be used as a listening and play-along tool.
00220005 Book 1 – Book/CD Pack $24.95
00220006 Book 2 – Book/CD Pack $24.95

THE PATH TO JAZZ IMPROVISATION
by Emile and Laura De Cosmo
This fascinating jazz instruction book offers an innovative, scholarly approach to the art of improvisation. It includes in-depth analysis and lessons about: cycle of fifths • diatonic cycle • overtone series • pentatonic scale • harmonic and melodic minor scale • polytonal order of keys • blues and bebop scales • modes • and more.
00310904 ....$14.95

THE SOURCE
THE DICTIONARY OF CONTEMPORARY AND TRADITIONAL SCALES
by Steve Barta
This book serves as an informative guide for people who are looking for good, solid information regarding scales, chords, and how they work together. It provides right and left hand fingerings for scales, chords, and complete inversions. Includes over 20 different scales, each written in all 12 keys.
00240885 ....$12.95

21 BEBOP EXERCISES
by Steve Rawlins
This book/CD pack is both a warm-up collection and a manual for bebop phrasing. Its tasty and sophisticated exercises will help you develop your proficiency with jazz interpretation. It concentrates on practice in all twelve keys – moving higher by half-step – to help develop dexterity and range. The companion CD includes all of the exercises in 12 keys.
00315341 Book/CD Pack $17.95

THE WOODSHEDDING SOURCE BOOK
by Emile De Cosmo
Rehearsing with this method daily will improve technique, reading ability, rhythmic and harmonic vocabulary, eye/finger coordination, endurance, range, theoretical knowledge, and listening skills – all of which lead to superior improvisational skills.
00842000 C Instruments $19.95

Prices, contents & availability subject to change without notice.